Original title:

Swaying Palms and Ocean Dreams

Copyright © 2025 Creative Arts Management OÜ
All rights reserved.

Author: Matthew Whitaker
ISBN HARDBACK: 978-1-80581-501-3
ISBN PAPERBACK: 978-1-80581-028-5
ISBN EBOOK: 978-1-80581-501-3

Fragments of a Summer Dream

Underneath the coconut trees,
A crab stole my sandwich with ease.
He danced on the sand with a flick,
I thought, 'Was that just a trick?'

Waves laughed as they crashed and rolled,
While seagulls squawked, oh so bold.
I built a castle with grand peaks,
But the tide claimed it within weeks.

Sunburned noses and big sun hats,
Chasing gulls, we looked like rats.
A fish jumped out, stole my drink,
I never knew they had that sneak.

As twilight came, we gathered round,
With jokes and laughter, summer found.
A dolphin flipped, the sea breeze blew,
And I wondered if they had a clue!

The Whirl of Vacation Wishes

The suitcase exploded, what a sight,
Socks and snacks took a wild flight.
Sunscreen danced in the summer air,
While flip-flops played tag without a care.

The beach ball rolled away to the sand,
With a life of its own, it made a stand.
Ice cream cones formed a sticky crew,
As seagulls plotted mischief too.

Echoing Laughter in the Breeze

We built a castle, tall and grand,
But waves had other plans, oh man!
The throne washed away with a laugh and a splash,
As crabs marched by in a crustacean flash.

Bikini tops flew like kites in the air,
While sunburns appeared without a care.
Giggles echoed, carried by the tide,
In a world where worries take a ride.

Chasing Sunsets and Salty Winds

With lounge chairs upside down, we grinned,
As kites tangled high with a whirlwind.
The sunset flared, like a painter's brush,
While sand got stuck in quite a rush.

A dolphin popped up, said, 'Join the fun!'
We waved and tripped, fell flat on the run.
Laughter bubbled with every wave,
In a coastal circus, oh how we rave!

The Allure of Boundless Waters

The boat rocked gently, but wait, oh no!
The fishing line tangled, a clownfish show.
My hat took flight, into the blue haze,
As waves giggled, lost in their plays.

We caught nothing but a basket of snacks,
And swam with the fish, not expecting flak.
Each splash a story, of joy and delight,
In this sea of laughter, everything's right.

Dancing Leaves at Dusk

When leaves do the tango, they twist with grace,
A squirrel in a tux, a nut on his face.
They twirl and they spin, on the breeze they soar,
I laugh as they dance, what a silly chore!

A breeze brings a chuckle, rustles the trees,
While branches play tag with the buzzing bees.
The sun takes a bow, as night starts to creep,
The leaves whisper secrets, while we're fast asleep.

Rhythm of the Coastal Breeze

The wind throws a party, invites all the shells,
A crab working DJ, with his funky jells.
He spins up some tunes with a snap and a clap,
While seagulls groove along, flapping their flap!

Each wave joins the dance, a splash and a spin,
The sand takes a selfie, with a wide, goofy grin.
A fish jumps the beat, in a splash of delight,
As the sun keeps on shining, oh what a sight!

Secrets Beneath the Sea

Down below the surface, where fish tell their tales,
A crab spills the gossip, while eel wiggles sails.
The turtles all chuckle at the clownfish show,
While octopuses tango, all in a row!

A treasure chest laughs, it's got jokes galore,
With pirates' lost socks, it can hardly store.
The seaweed sways gently, like it's in on the joke,
While jellyfish giggle, in a glowing cloak.

Echoes of Sun-Kissed Shores

The sun seeks the sand for a warm, soft hug,
While flip-flops start sliding, all snug as a bug.
A dog rolls in seaweed, makes friends with a crab,
And laughter erupts from the beachy fab!

Balloons float away, like thoughts on a breeze,
While kids build tall castles, shaky at these.
But waves crash their plans, with a splashy delight,
As everyone giggles, what a silly sight!

Canopy of Light Beneath the Skies

Beneath the sun, we laugh and play,
A seagull steals my sandwich away.
Shells like jewels, we gather in heaps,
While crabs crawl over, causing loud squeaks.

The breeze tickles our sunburnt skin,
We race the waves, we cheer, we win!
But oh, that wave was not my friend,
It flipped me backward, oh, what a blend!

Serenity in the Seafoam's Embrace

Flotation devices in vibrant hues,
Like life rings tossed in a game of blues.
We paddle around in the cool, clear sea,
While dolphins do flips, laughing with glee.

Sunblock on noses, a comical sight,
We giggle at seagulls that take their flight.
Caught in a web of sand and seaweed,
A dance-off ensues; it's silly indeed!

Dreams Beneath a Coconut Canopy

Coconuts drop, we dodge and dive,
Cracking open a drink, oh, we feel alive!
Umbrella drinks make us sway and sing,
While laughter and joy is the real king.

We search for treasure under the sand,
Only to find a flip-flop so grand.
But wait, what's that? A crab in disguise?
It pinches my toe! Surprise, oh surprise!

The Languid Dance of Tropical Nights

Under the stars with a ukulele's strum,
We stomp our feet, oh, what a fun drum!
Fireflies twinkle, like disco lights,
We whirl around, giggling through the nights.

Mango snacks stick to our faces bright,
As we sway like the breeze, full of delight.
Dancing the night away, carefree and bold,
Remembering stories that never get old!

Breezes in an Island Reverie

A llama in sunglasses struts with flair,
While seagulls gossip, without a care.
Tropical drinks with umbrellas swirl,
As the pineapple tries to dance and twirl.

The coconuts laugh, they're quite the crowd,
Poking fun at the shy cloud.
Bikini-clad crabs play a tune,
Under the watch of a silly raccoon.

Moonlit Reflections on Aqua Sands

A crab wearing beads sashays with glee,
While a starfish complains of no coffee.
Moonbeams twinkle in a magical chase,
Tickling the toes of a smiling sea bass.

A jellyfish breaks out in a jig,
As dolphins laugh, doing a big gig.
The waves keep splashing, what a sight,
Punching the shore like a child in flight.

Tranquil Horizons Awash with Light

A pelican wears a little bow tie,
While fish swim past with an inquisitive eye.
Bananas in hammocks, oh what a treat,
Debating if they'll dance or just take a seat.

The sun does a limbo, bends down low,
As otters juggle, putting on a show.
A boat with a lazy cat on the prow,
Snoozes away while the world says wow!

The Gentle Kiss of Dusk on Water

As the sun gets sleepy, it yawns and glows,
A turtle in shades acts like he knows.
Mermaids giggle, with laughter grand,
Playing tag with a lazy sandman.

Crickets start singing their nighttime song,
While a lone gopher dances along.
The breeze whispers secrets, all in fun,
As the day bids farewell, now the night's begun.

Portraits of Paradise

In shades of green with a quirky cheer,
The coconut fell, and someone disappeared.
Beach towels tangled like fish in a net,
The seagulls gossip with nary a fret.

A crab wore sunglasses, sassy and bold,
Strutting by sunbathers, his story retold.
Flip-flops were dancing, a silly parade,
While ice cream cones melted, a colorful cascade.

The surfboard's a whale? At least that's the claim,
Riding the waves, they both play the same game.
Tropical drinks with umbrellas stand proud,
As laughter erupts, echoing loud.

So come, take a snapshot of this joyous spree,
Where mischief and sun mix with a splash of glee.
Every moment a canvas, brushed wildly with cheer,
In this world of laughter, let's give a big cheer!

Dreams Drifted in the Surf

A rubber duck floats, what a sight to behold,
Waving to jellyfish in colors so bold.
Surfboards are crowded, all patient in line,
While sunburned tourists say, "This is divine!"

The waves did the cha-cha, so wild and so free,
While lifeguards were giggling, not guarding the sea.
Beach umbrellas tangoed, a wobbly show,
As sunscreen battles sparked, 'twas a slippery blow.

Popcorn in hand, a flock of birds conspire,
To snatch every kernel, their goal is higher.
Beachballs exploded with glitter and glee,
As kids built sandcastles, a charming decree.

Floating the tide with an over-the-top grin,
The ocean waves whispered, let the fun begin.
So dreams ride the surf, in a whimsical spin,
Where laughter and sunshine create the best win!

Shadows of Coconut Trees

Coconuts dancing, what a silly scene,
Flapping their leaves, all dressed in bright green.
Their shadows stretched long, like lazy cats napping,
While crabs plotted heists, the beach scene unwrapping.

With flip-flops a-clapping and seagulls on guard,
The shadows spun stories, both funny and hard.
A picnic gone wild, ants in a race,
As dogs ponder life with a perplexed face.

The sun painted laughter, a colorful hue,
As kites took to flight, "Catch me if you can too!"
In the coconut grove, where giggles are found,
Every shadow a secret, no stranger around.

So let's dance with the breeze and sway to the tune,
Where shadows get lost in the light of the moon.
The trees share their gossip, soft whispers in glee;
In this realm of delight, come join the spree!

Dancing Shadows on the Sand

With footprints like scribbles in warm golden dust,
The sun whispered secrets, in it we trust.
A dog in a tutu, quite ready to prance,
Chasing his tail in a whimsical dance.

The shadows grew taller as sunset drew near,
The beach balls were bouncing, a jubilant cheer.
A piña colada took a dive in the sand,
While laughter erupted, life was so grand.

Shovels and buckets sat idle and sore,
While tiny toes wiggled and begged for more.
The waves played hide and seek, splashing in jubilee,
As the tide took their woes, setting all free.

So we twirl through the dusk, under stars that ignite,
With happiness swirling, it feels just so right.
Dance with the shadows, let giggles expand,
In this playful adventure, a jubilant land!

Serene Horizons in Motion

The trees dance with a silly twist,
As if they're caught in a morning mist.
Waves giggle as they tickle the shore,
While seagulls laugh and beg for more.

The sun wears shades, a jester bright,
Joking with clouds in the afternoon light.
The breeze joins in with a playful cheer,
Whispering secrets that only we hear.

A crab in a tux takes a wobbly stride,
While fish in bow ties swim side by side.
Watermelon slices float all around,
In a world where humor knows no bound.

With each splash and chuckle we find our way,
In this paradise, let's dance and play.
For laughter is found in the sun's warm glow,
Where the quirky tales of nature flow.

Lullabies of the Lagoon

Bubbles pop like cheerful songs,
As frogs croak out their playful throngs.
The moon holds a grin, broad and wide,
As wiggly fish take a glowing ride.

Driftwood boats made from toast and bread,
Float on dreams where silly things tread.
Mischief brews in the shallow bay,
As crabs conspire to steal fish away.

The water tickles our toes with glee,
While egrets strut like they own the sea.
And every splash, a giggle unleashed,
In this lagoon, we are famished beasts.

So let's sway with joy till the sun is high,
With lullabies of laughter under the sky.
For in this wet wonderland, we'll never tire,
As giggles float higher, ever inspir'd.

Canopy of Stars Above

Stars wink down with a playful light,
Bouncing off waves that shimmer bright.
The crickets sing in rhythm, quite bold,
While the ocean murmurs secrets untold.

A turtle dons a cap for style's sake,
Pretending to be grand, make no mistake!
While jellyfish twirl in a dazzling show,
Revealing their disco moves in a flow.

Laughter drifts through the silky night,
As shells hold secrets in moonlit flight.
With each twinkle, a giggle is born,
In the realm where laughter and stars are worn.

So let's toast to the antics, wild and free,
Under a sky where we all wish to be.
With humor igniting our hearts to soar,
In this celestial dream, we'll forever explore.

Cascade of Waves and Wonder

Waves crash in fits of comedic flair,
Like clowns taking turns to dance in the air.
A beach ball bounces with glee on the tide,
As laughter rides high on each playful glide.

Each splash is a chuckle, a tickle of fun,
As sunbathers giggle, their worries undone.
A seagull makes off with a sandwich feast,
While children chase shadows of an invisible beast.

The snorkelers bubble in underwater play,
Hilarious fish swim their own silly way.
And the sandcastles boast of their impressive might,
Till the next wave declares they've lost the fight.

In this crescendo of joy and delight,
Where giggles and waves fuse in the night,
Let's ride the humor on this current of cheer,
In our cascade of wonder, let's persevere.

Haven of Salty Air

In the breeze, a sandwich flies,
With seagulls' laughter in the skies.
Pineapple hats upon our heads,
As we trip over beachside beds.

Flip-flops squeak, a funny sound,
Dancing crabs feel quite renowned.
We sip our drinks, umbrellas tall,
While sunscreen stings—oh, what a fall!

Sand gets everywhere, oh my gosh,
On sandwiches and in my frosh.
Laughter bubbles, waves go splish,
Watermelon's the real fish dish!

With every splash, a clownish face,
Belly flops take over this place.
We swim like whales, we swim like fish,
And giggle at our sandy bliss!

The sun begins its slow retreat,
Tanning creams make life quite sweet.
But watch your step, don't trip on boats,
Or join the jelly's goggle floats!

Twilight's Gentle Murmurs

The sun sets low, the crickets sing,
My mate forgot the burger thing.
Flip-flops squeak, we dance with glee,
While the ocean plays hide and seek.

Starfish chat with bottle caps,
The moonlight offers funny laps.
We try to catch a breeze so light,
But seagulls rally for a bite!

Mismatched socks on sandy feet,
Waves tease us with their playful beat.
Our laughter rolls on ocean hums,
As gulls tell tales of bread crumbs.

The sky's a canvas, orange, pink,
We joke about a shark in sync.
But who would care? We've got our snacks,
And goofy dances, happy tracks!

Tranquil Moments by the Water

We dip our toes, and what a sight,
A crab does the cha-cha in the night.
Lemonades spill; who said we're cool?
We're the funny folks near the pool!

Banana boats down the shore glide,
But wait—are they really just a ride?
We drift like driftwood on the waves,
Cracking jokes like silly knaves.

Our beach ball flies into a local's grill,
"Hey, watch it!" they shout, but we're just thrill!
Noses sunburned, we wear the red,
As laughter rolls, good vibes spread.

The ocean whispers, we all agree,
Nothing beats this jubilee.
So here we roast and roast some more,
With sand between our toes, we soar!

Murmurs of the Tropical Isle

Underneath the palm tree's mode,
My drink explodes, a fruity load!
Summer hats flying in the breeze,
As laughter dances with such ease.

Tanned legs tangled in the chairs,
Waves whisper secrets, silly fares.
To seashells, we tell our tales of grace,
While crabs sneak sneak peeks at our space.

With coconut boats set to sail,
We paddle like we're on a trail.
But splash! Oh no, we tipped it right,
Floating snacks take off in flight!

With toes in sand, our giggles roar,
Getting sunburned thanks to lore.
But no complaints, just frosty cheer,
As beach balls bounce the whole way here!

Reverie in the Island Breeze

On a beach with sand so fine,
I tripped over my drink, divine!
The seagulls laughed, oh what a show,
As I chased my hat that wouldn't go.

With coconuts tossed in the air,
I danced like no one was there.
The sun said, 'You really can't sing!'
But I smiled and wore my floral bling.

My flip-flops flipped far off my feet,
They landed where sea monsters meet.
With a splash and a giggle, I made a dive,
Chasing fish that looked quite alive.

As the sun dipped low, I cracked a joke,
The tide rolled in, and so did smoke.
The laughter echoed, waves joined in,
This island life, a playful spin!

Tapestry of the Deep Blue

Floating on a floatie grand,
I yelled, 'I'm the king of this land!'
But the wind gave my crown a toss,
And I ended up swimming with a moss.

The fish wore masks like they were cool,
I swear they'd laugh if I was a fool.
'Come dance with us,' they seemed to say,
I flailed my arms, and splashed away.

Sunscreen battles on my back,
Streaks of white, I felt like a snack.
The crabs on the shore began to cheer,
As I tried to dance without any fear.

With each wave that rolled and crashed,
I treasured the tales of taught and trashed.
The ocean smiled as it wrung my hair,
In this wacky world, I found my flair!

Wanderlust Under Palm Fronds

Under canopies swaying at night,
I dreamed I could dance with delight.
But a bug said, 'Not so fast, my friend!'
And my flip turned into a tornado bend.

Tiki torches flickered in glee,
As I ran for the last slice of brie.
The laughter rumbled, as I marched,
Tripped on roots, my dignity parched.

I spotted a crab in a tiny hat,
He wiggled and jiggled, oh imagine that!
Took him for salsa, to my surprise,
He danced like a pro, right before my eyes.

The stars above whispered their secrets,
While I ignored all my defeats.
With friends by my side, and laughter loud,
This whimsical night, I felt so proud!

Radiance of a Seaside Repose

With a towel flung in the sky,
I claimed my throne, oh my oh my!
But a breeze snatched my ice cream away,
As I shouted, 'Return, you crafty sway!'

The sun got sassy, pulling strings,
While I fumbled with a hula hoop's flings.
A seagull perched, judging my form,
But I stayed cool in this weather warm.

Playing frisbee was a great disgrace,
I sent it flying into someone's face.
Giggling kids yelled, 'It's a game!'
I waved back, feeling quite the same.

As the day faded into a paint of peach,
I clutched my drink, it's a fabulous reach!
With friends and laughter, we made a pledge,
To forever meet where waves did edge!

Captured Moments in Salty Air

I saw a crab in a tiny hat,
Trying to dance like a silly cat.
The seagulls laughed and joined the fray,
While folks just pointed, in pure dismay.

A fish in flip-flops dared to swim,
But tripped on seaweed, went in with a whim.
It flopped around, a live spectacle,
As beachgoers cheered, it was magical!

The sunscreen war was a sight to behold,
With one friend glistening, a nice shade of gold.
The others, all covered like buttered toast,
Declared beach antics were worth a boast.

Then came a wave, with laughter and glee,
As it swept up a sandwich, a poor casualty.
But everyone laughed, all worries erased,
Moments like these can't be replaced.

Footprints in the Whispering Sands

Tiny toes left prints so cute,
But then a wave made them all mute.
The little ones squealed, full of delight,
As their precious marks vanished from sight.

A jellyfish danced like it owned the place,
While kids made faces, grimacing with grace.
They said, "What's the deal with its jiggly jig?"
"I think it's just auditioning for a gig!"

Shells in a pile showed a merry tale,
Of critters that wandered and set off to sail.
But one sly crab claimed them for homes,
And evicted the seagulls who wandered and roamed.

With kites in the sky and candies in hand,
We all chuckled, just a merry band.
The footprints might fade, but the laughs will stay,
In this sandy adventure, come what may!

The Embrace of Wind and Water

The ocean waved like an old friend's hand,
Trying to tickle, oh isn't it grand?
And I dodged a splash, like a whimsical game,
While the waves shouted back, "Come join in the fame!"

I built a sandcastle, tall as a tree,
Until a gust blew it down, oh me!
"It needed more turrets," a child said with cheer,
As I laughed at my kingdom, gone in a smear.

A dolphin jumped high, showed off its flair,
While nearby a kid lost his cotton candy layer.
The sweet treat stuck on a pelican's beak,
Turning the scene into comedy chic.

As sunset painted the sky rosy bright,
We all shared tales, from day until night.
Though sand stuck to sunscreen, and laughs filled the air,
With every moment, we knew we were rare.

Whispers of the Tide

The tide brought whispers, soft as a breeze,
Enticing a limpet to dance with ease.
But every time it tried to look slick,
It ended up stuck in a salty little tick.

With surfboards aglow and laughter on tap,
A kid made a splash, while filling a gap.
And the dog chased waves with such silly flair,
While everyone chuckled and tossed back their hair.

A friendly shark with a grin so wide,
Decided to join in the beachside ride.
But folks just shrieked, in a flurry and flash,
As it turned out to be just another prank splash.

As dusk slowly crept, the lanterns would shine,
We gathered around, sipping drinks, feeling fine.
And though sand was everywhere, quite the parade,
These echoes of laughter would never just fade.

Celestial Conversations at Dusk

Beneath the stars, we chatter loud,
About the seagulls and the clouds.
A fish jumped high, or was it a cat?
I swear it wore a sun hat!

With waves that giggle, and breeze that jokes,
We debate the antics of silly folks.
The moon winks down as I try to dance,
Tripping over my own two pants!

A shell comes by, with a story to tell,
Of mermaid parties and seaweed smells.
We laugh and laugh, till the sand does stick,
I think that crab just tried to do a trick!

As dolphins peek with a wink and a smile,
Their graceful flips make it worth the while.
So here's to the night, with its laughter so bright,
Where fish wear sunglasses, and all feels just right!

The Essence of Shorebound Serenity

On sandy shores, where giggles fly,
We build castles that scrape the sky.
While seagulls join with a raucous cheer,
I swear that one just sipped my beer!

The tide rolls in, wearing shoes of foam,
While crabs play tag, then scuttle home.
I chase a wave that chose to retreat,
And end up tangled in seaweed's seat!

A lobster stuck to a beach ball blast,
Said, 'I'm a star, just look at my cast!'
We laugh at the fish and the presents they bring,
Singing songs in a very fishy fling!

So let's toast to sand and the sun above,
Where laughter sparkles like a fish loves a shove.
Each moment we share is tied with a string,
Let's dance with the tide, let our joy take wing!

Sunbeams and Ocean Hues

As sunbeams tickle the surface bright,
We try to surf but take off in flight.
I splashed my buddy, he splashed me back,
Who knew a wave could have such a knack?

With every ripple, a laugh erupts,
While jellyfish play lyrical chucks.
I caught a wave and wobbled in grace,
Right into a sea dog, what a face!

The sun makes us gleam like treasures untold,
Each glimmer of joy has a story bold.
The ocean whispers secrets and sighs,
While a clam plays hide and seek with its fries!

We dance in delight, our hearts in the blue,
With laughter enough for each salty crew.
So here's to the fun, the sun, and the play,
Let's swim with our laughs, come what may!

A Driftwood's Odyssey

A driftwood log rolled up with sass,
Claimed it was once a sailing class.
'Taught turtles all the tricks of the tide!'
Whoa there, buddy, take that with pride!

With barnacles dressed in a glitter parade,
This log tells tales, a real charade.
'We sailed past sharks for a silly thrill,'
'And dodged a whale that tried to chill!'

As kids make wishes on its rugged form,
It waves goodbye in a crafty charm.
For every splash, there's a secret surprise,
Like a disco party for all sea life flies!

So let's hear it for journey's sweet flair,
For driftwood dreams that float in the air.
Their laughs echo softly through waves that gleam,
A hilarious log with a whimsical dream!

Fragrance of Saline Secrets

I caught a whiff of fishy flair,
A crab scuttled by with stylish hair,
He wore a hat, oh what a sight,
While seagulls honked, they took a bite.

The beach ball rolled, a daring feat,
Chasing after it, I lost my seat,
My toes in sand and laughter loud,
A seagull landed, oh so proud.

Walking sideways like a crab parade,
Trying not to slip, I'm quite afraid,
I yell, "Watch out!" to all my friends,
They trip, and then the giggle ends.

The ocean waves throw parties too,
Each splash a jest, a joke or two,
I dance with jellyfish, such a tease,
Who knew sea life loved to please!

Meditations by the Water's Edge

Sitting here, I ponder life,
Why did my sandwich start a strife?
The tide rolled in, my lunch was wet,
And now my bliss, I can't forget.

The starfish giggle, all in a row,
As I try yoga, to and fro,
My balance lost, I drop and flop,
The waves just laugh, they never stop.

With seagulls swooping, like they own,
A beach towel throne, my fuzzy zone,
They feng shui-ed my snacks away,
Real meditations, come what may.

I try to think of life's great truth,
But all I get is salty youth,
So here I sit, with crunching sounds,
Meditating on my munching rounds.

Ballet of the Blowing Palms

In this dance, the breezes waltz,
While coconuts get ready for faults,
They sway and twirl with cupped big hands,
Catching sunrays, perfecting strands.

I tried to join their leafy show,
But tripped on roots, an absurd glow,
The palms just chuckled, whispering cheer,
While I laid tangled, but with no fear.

The sun was bright, a disco ball,
Reflecting on waves that rise and fall,
I donned a leaf, my costume grand,
A pirate in a palm's lush band.

I danced with zeal, yet lost my step,
While crabs rolled by, they laughed, they leapt,
The palms applauded, in rustling tones,
In a ballet where all are clones.

Colors of the Sea's Embrace

There's purple jelly in my drink,
With lemon slice that made me think,
Is it a beverage or a pet?
A jiggly friend? I can't quite bet!

The turquoise waves come crashing fast,
With frothy laughter, unsurpassed,
They tickle my toes, oh what a tease,
I spill my drink - it was a breeze!

Golden sands stretched far and near,
As I worked hard to make seashells clear,
But every time I'd find a prize,
It slipped away, oh how it flies!

The sunset sprinkled hues just right,
While crabs invited me to their night,
A party where all colors scream,
And beach fun dances like a dream!

Mystique of the Moonlit Beach

The waves giggle under the light,
Sandcastles joke, 'We'll last tonight!'
A crab in a tux tries to dance,
Just a little sideways, what a chance!

Seagulls caw secrets in the air,
A dolphin flips, without a care.
Shells whisper tales of moonlit whim,
While the tide pulls in on a jellyfish swim.

The stars chuckle at silly sights,
As we dig for treasures in the night.
A flip-flop flies, gets caught by a breeze,
And I'm just wishing for some frozen peas!

With friends who laugh until we ache,
We share the tales that we will make.
By morning, we'll wonder what went wrong,
But tonight, oh tonight, we laugh along!

Parables of the Pacific

Waves roll in with stories to tell,
Of fish who thought they'd swim so well.
The sand is warm, the jokes are bright,
With every splash, we gather delight.

A pelican dives for some old fries,
While a sea turtle looks up, all surprise.
A beach ball bounces, lands on a crab,
Who winks and shuffles, life's quite fab!

Flip-flops missing, but who knows where?
The tide keeps secrets, the sun's our glare.
We dance on the shore, oh, what a sight,
As waves crash with laughter, pure delight!

At sunset, we'll share all the fishy tales,
Of octopuses wearing old sailor veils.
So hold up your drinks, let's toast to the night,
In this paradise where humor takes flight!

Synchronicity of Tides

The ocean winks, a playful tease,
As surfers tumble with the breeze.
Seashells clatter, join the fun,
Making jokes until we're done.

Mermaids giggle, in waves they sway,
Teaching dolphins how to play.
A lighthouse giggles, shines so bright,
Guiding us home on this silly night.

A sand crab wears a starfish hat,
Looking for a cool spot to chat.
Our group of friends in fits of laughter,
Can't recall what we were after!

With night closing in, we seek a treat,
Ice cream cones are hard to beat.
Let's make a toast to the whimsical tides,
Where laughter and joy are our best guides!

Caresses of Soft Currents

Gentle breezes in our hair,
As we splash and butcher a dare.
An octopus claps at our grand show,
While seahorses dance, putting on a glow.

With buckets and shovels, we dig so deep,
Creating wonders, not worth a peep.
But the gulls fly low, they know the score,
And snatch our lunch — oh, we need more!

Sunburns are coded messages from the light,
Telling us, 'Stay out of sight!'
But we're too busy crafting our dreams,
With waves crashing in the in-betweens.

So here's to the tide's humor and grace,
Each soft current, a warm embrace.
In this paradise that teases and beams,
We'll laugh till we wake from our ocean dreams!

Refuge in Driftwood Shadows

Underneath the twisted driftwood,
Whispers tell of crabs in a feud.
The seagulls squawk a silly tune,
As sandcastles melt like a cartoon.

Turtles wearing shades take a stroll,
Dancing sideways, they rock and roll.
A starfish wearing a funky hat,
Winks to a clam, 'How about that?'

Coconuts giggle as they drop,
From palm rooftops—oh, such a plop!
A pelican, with flair so bold,
Will steal your fries; we all know, he's gold.

In shadows deep where the laughter swells,
Echoes of fun in the ocean's bells.
If you listen close, you can hear the cheer,
In driftwood's refuge, we laugh without fear.

The Dance of Forgotten Shores

On a beach where nobody cares,
Dance with ghosts who lost their pairs.
A jellyfish in disco lights,
Flashes moves that reach new heights.

The hermit crabs line up to groove,
In perfect sync, their shells approve.
Shellfish cheer with polished smiles,
As they strut down the sandy aisles.

Old shoes thrown in from years of fun,
Join the party, they've finally won.
Waves giggle as they splash away,
While seashells giggle in sun's warm play.

But watch your toes, the wave might tease,
Pulling you in with a playful squeeze.
In forgotten shores, there's room for all,
Where laughter echoes, and giggles enthrall.

Bliss in the Crashing Surf

A walrus wearing sunglasses wide,
Slips on seaweed, takes a ride.
Surfboards made from old tin cans,
Race the waves like eager fans.

Octopuses juggle beach balls high,
With arms that stretch toward the sky.
Crabs in capes, they flap and play,
Making new friends at the end of the day.

Sandy socks covered in sand,
Pretend they're slipping, just as planned.
With every splash, the laughter grows,
As sea turtles join in the shows.

A dolphin cracks jokes that make you snort,
While fishes collaborate—oh, what sport!
In the crashing surf, joy bursts free,
With humor riding the waves, just like the sea.

Merging Horizons of Sea and Sky

Where the sun dips low in a grin,
And seagulls hunt for discarded din.
Kites tangled in a fisherman's pole,
Laugh as they dance, out of control.

A crab wearing a bright bowtie,
Shuffles past with a wink and a sigh.
Beach towels flutter in the breeze,
Like friendship flags among the trees.

Clouds above look like fluffy cakes,
As waves below create silly wakes.
The pelicans plot their next big prank,
While sunbathers nap, unaware of the tank.

As night approaches, laughter fades,
But memories painted in golden shades.
A toast to the fun, the tide now ties,
In the merging hues of sea and skies.

Dreams Carried by the Waves

The seagull steals my sandwich, oh what a fuss,
My picnic gone, I taste salty rust.
A crab walks by, wearing a tiny hat,
I swear he winked, that sneaky brat!

The tide rolls in with a goofy grin,
Tickling my toes, where do I begin?
Surfboards tumble; it's quite a sight,
Who knew catching waves meant losing a fight!

A jellyfish dances, oh so spry,
I poke it gently—did it just sigh?
The sun smiles down, with a cheery beam,
While I wrestle blend-a-mangle ice cream!

With laughter echoing through the salty air,
I chase crabs 'round, without a care.
Dreams bubble up like foam on the shore,
Life's a beach; I couldn't ask for more!

Fables of Coastal Existence

A clam's got secrets, it's stuck on a phrase,
Whispers of pearls in the sun's bright rays.
A turtle in shades, cool as can be,
He's a surfer dude, just waiting for me.

Seashells are gossiping, sharing old tales,
Of fish who wore boots and sailing with whales.
A dolphin does jumps with a flourish so fine,
Sipping on seaweed, he's feeling divine!

The sandflakes giggle, all golden and bright,
Competing for space beneath my flip-flop fight.
While waves clap hands in a bubbly song,
Fables of fun where we all belong!

Oh, beach chairs wrestle in a windy spree,
They take down my drink—what a crazy plea!
Life on the coast is full of sweet strife,
Where laughter's the treasure, and joy is the life.

Journey of the Water's Whisper

Little fish sing about their daily trips,
While dolphins giggle, making tight flips.
The sea tells jokes in a bubbling tease,
As crabs hold court under swaying trees.

A starfish auditions for a Broadway scene,
With eight-legged moves, it's quite the routine!
Bubbles burst forth with a pop and a cheer,
As I float on by, with my tilt-a-whirl beer.

The boat's got a mind, it wants to go fast,
But I'm holding on tight, oh, this ride won't last!
The anchors laugh loudly, saying "Not today!"
I steer with my toes, come what may!

Clouds join the fun, look silly and bright,
As my towel flies off, what a comical sight!
Each wave's a joke, splashing laughter around,
In a journey of whispers, where joy can be found.

Heartbeats of the Sea

The ocean's pulse is a quirky beat,
As jellybeans dance on my sandy seat.
A whale takes selfies, it aims to impress,
Saying, "Look at my fluke—it's a real success!"

Seashells spinning tales of beachtime cheer,
While surfboards argue, "I'm the true steer!"
A piña colada takes a stroll by the shore,
"Stay cool," it insists, "and let's party some more!"

The gulls are gossiping, it's all the rage,
Reporting who's surfing on the next stage.
With flips and tumbles, they take to the sky,
While I try to balance with a hot dog pie!

In rhythmic rhythm, the coastlines combine,
With giggles of waves singing, "You're always divine."
Let's toast with a splash, as the sun dips down,
In the heart of the sea, laughter wears the crown!

Chasing Sunsets

On golden sands we run around,
Our feet make prints without a sound.
The sun's a ball, we're full of cheer,
Chasing shadows, never fear.

With ice cream cones that start to drip,
We laugh so hard, we start to trip.
The gulls are giggling up above,
They know the secret: life is love.

We roll and tumble on the beach,
While waves come in, they seem to reach.
Splashing water, like a dance,
Who knew that sand could make us prance?

As night unfolds, we spot a star,
We dream of places near and far.
But first, a snack, let's take a bite,
Chasing sunsets feels so right!

Embracing Horizons

With arms outstretched, we shout with glee,
The horizon sings, come play with me!
Here comes a breeze, it's full of fun,
We dance like waves, all said and done.

Our kites are flying high and wide,
While laughter echoes, we can't hide.
The sun winks down with a playful wink,
Amongst the clouds, we jump and think.

Spinning in circles, we might get dizzy,
But with each giggle, it's far from busy.
We, like fools, chase after light,
Embracing moments, pure delight.

As day turns to night, we look around,
And find our joy is truly profound.
With every wave that hits the shore,
We know in our hearts, there's always more!

The Calm Within the Wild Waters

In wild waters, we find our thrill,
A splash here and there, a little chill.
We paddle our way, oh what a sight,
While fish jump up with all their might.

The rafts are floating, we're quite a crew,
With oars in hand, we'll conquer blue.
A seagull steals our lunch with style,
But we just laugh and stretch a while.

With waves that crash and tides that tease,
We send out bubbles on the breeze.
Oh, watch out now, a wave so grand!
We squeal and splash—here goes our sand!

Yet in the chaos, there's peace to find,
A giggly heart, a joyful mind.
Through whirlpools of laughter, we drift away,
In wild waters, we wish to stay.

Echoes of Laughter on Summer Breezes

On summer days, the sun's a clown,
It paints the sky in orange gown.
We run so fast, we fly so high,
With silly hats, oh me, oh my!

The breeze whispers secrets, soft and sweet,
As we dance along with little feet.
And bubbles float like dreams in air,
Pop! Pop! Oh, we haven't a care!

The swing set creaks with laughter bright,
As fireflies twinkle, a lovely sight.
We're the playwrights of this sunny play,
With goofy giggles, we seize the day.

As evening falls, we share a grin,
With echoes of laughter still within.
Under the stars, the night's our stage,
We write our stories, turn the page!

Tidal Dances in the Warm Embrace

In the warm embrace of sunny cheer,
We do the tidal dance, oh dear!
A splash of water, we twirl around,
Like silly fish, we're ocean-bound.

The crabs are watching, snapping claws,
As we forget all of life's laws.
With goofy steps, we shimmy low,
We're dancers now, putting on a show!

Flip-flops flying, towels in a twist,
We leap and bound, how could we resist?
The seaweed's green and full of flair,
Tidal movements, everywhere!

As laughter rings, the tides will change,
We find sweet joy in the strange.
With sun-soaked skin and hearts aglow,
In this embrace, we'll sway and flow.

Poetry Found Beneath Sunlit Canopies

Under bright leaves, I take a snooze,
A crab steps over, wearing my shoes.
He tells me stories of the tide's great pranks,
While seagulls squawk about their wild shanks.

The coconut falls, a surprise on my head,
I leap up startled, and nearly fled.
The sand shifts beneath my flip-flopped feet,
A dance floor, where I trip in the heat.

Laughter erupts as I roll in the sand,
A friendship with sandcastles so grand.
Now they all laugh, as they watch me don,
A hat made of shells, I'm the king of this dawn!

In the shade, we sip juice, my friends and I,
While a crab serves drinks with a wink and a sigh.
Under the canopies, where joy interweaves,
We craft our tales, like lines from our leaves.

Landscapes of Liquid Dreams

Waves play tag with the colorful surfboards,
Making sea foam jokes, breaking all the wards.
I ride the crest, with a squeal and a splash,
While dolphins chuckle, and clams tend to crash.

The sun's a cheeky thief, stealing my hat,
It dances away, as I shout and spat.
Fish giggle at my clumsy attempts,
While lobsters snicker at my sea-themed pretense.

In this aquatic circus, all play their part,
As I juggle my beach snacks, that's quite an art!
A seagull swoops down, being rather rude,
Takes my sandwich—what a comical feud!

Splashing about in a whimsical game,
Water fights start, and laughter's to blame.
With every wave that crashes and rolls,
We find little treasures, and share silly goals.

Nostalgia in the Fresh Sea Air

Salty breezes whisper tales from the past,
Old flip-flops wandering, hoping they last.
A childhood kite flies, tangled in dreams,
While crabs perform limbo, or so it seems.

Seashells tell secrets, in colors so bright,
Each holds a story of day or of night.
I step on a squid, what a slippery mess,
It glares up at me, with a tentacle press!

Bucket in hand, I'm here to create,
A castle with moats that will surely await.
But the tide has a plan to sweep it away,
Leaving me giggling, a clown in the spray.

The ocean's my canvas, and laughter's my brush,
Painting memories in a bubbling hush.
Each splash a reminder to enjoy and embrace,
The funny moments that time can't erase.

The Allure of Shoreline Serenity

A beach ball bounces, escaping my clasp,
Chasing it down, oh what a gasp!
Seagulls overhead, squawk a funny tune,
While a starfish grins under the bright afternoon.

Sandcastles rise, but they don't stay still,
Waves play their games, oh what a thrill!
A sand dollar whispers, "Look at my style,"
I reply with a jig, and it flashes a smile.

Flat as a pancake, I lie on the shore,
Sunscreen a war paint, my body's all sore.
But oh, the giggles from sunburned friends,
We swear we'll remember, as the laughter never ends.

With beach towels spread out, our kingdom we claim,
We toast to our tumbles, in the sand's gentle frame.
So here's to the moments, the funny and free,
Where the shoreline whispers, let's just be silly!

Solitude under the Palms

A crab scuttles by, with a funny twirl,
He thinks he's the star, giving it a whirl.
Seagulls are laughing, sharing a snack,
While I sit in shade, plotting their attack.

The sun on my skin, feels like a roast,
I've got my drink, but it's just a ghost.
Ice melted away, it's just a tease,
I'm left with a splash, and a hint of freeze.

The breeze whispers jokes, oh what a feat,
Like tickling toes with warm, salty feet.
Laughter erupts from the nearby grill,
As someone drops buns, what a thrill!

Here I find joy, in the mischief of fate,
With laughter and crabs, I can hardly wait.
The beach is a stage where the oddballs play,
And I'm just an audience, lovin' the day!

Serenade of the Seaside

The waves hum a tune, a comedic flow,
While fish leap around, putting on a show.
I try to join in, but trip on my feet,
And splash in the surf, oh, isn't that neat?

A dolphin passes, it's giggling away,
Thinking I'm foolish, so lost in my play.
With fins that can flip, they twirl and tease,
While I practice my dance with the sand and the breeze.

Sunburned and silly, I wave at the skies,
Seashells are laughing, just look at their size!
They whisper their stories, so wise and so grand,
But I can't understand, it's all just quicksand.

Yet here's where I stand, in this comic delight,
Finding joy in the waves, as day turns to night.
The moon gives a wink, with a splash and a beam,
I'm off to my tent, 'cause this is a dream!

Kaleidoscope of Coral Reflections

Coral reefs giggle, in colors so bright,
As fish wear tiny hats, what a hilarious sight!
I tried to fit in, with a snorkel and glare,
But ended up tickled by a jellyfish's flair.

Each fin that flits by, tells a joke or two,
While I float like a log, oh, what could I do?
The seaweed sways, like it's had one too many,
Giggling along, probably thinks I'm a penny.

Shells chime in chorus, with puns from the deep,
While I'm puffing air, trying not to leap.
The world spins around, in a watery dance,
With a starfish that blushes, if only by chance.

So I wave to the critters, with laughter in tow,
As they bubble and gurgle, and put on a show.
The ocean's a circus, all wild and free,
And I'm just the clown, what a sight to see!

Embrace of the Wind's Caress

The wind waltzes in, with a playful swirl,
Tugging my hat, what a mischievous girl!
It fluffs up my shirt, gives my hair a spree,
While I chase after laughter, like it's calling me.

Kites dance above, in a colorful spree,
Who invited the seagulls? They're munching on brie!
I join in the fun, but I trip on the line,
And suddenly find that the air isn't mine.

Balloons float away, escaping my grasp,
While toes in the sand, I'm trying to clasp.
The sun beams a wink, and I surrender my frown,
To the joy of this chaos, this seaside clown.

So here in the wind, my heart finds its cheer,
In the comedy of waves, I have nothing to fear.
Just me and the sea, in this whimsical quest,
Where the laughs never end, and I'm feeling blessed!

Luminous Pathways by Moonlight

Under the glow of a silly moon,
Crabs dance wildly to a tuneless tune.
Sea stars giggle, twinkling bright,
While fish throw parties, a lively sight.

The waves wear costumes, all so strange,
A ballet of bubbles in a playful range.
Seagulls squawk jokes, high in the air,
While we build sandcastles beyond compare.

The tide decides it wants to play,
And sweeps our towels far away.
We chase it down, a funny sight,
Belly laughs echo through the night.

With sandy toes and salty cheer,
We dance like fools, without a fear.
The moon winks at our silly prance,
Reminding us life's a wacky dance.

Embracing the Coastal Charm

Shells all gather for a gossip spree,
Chit-chat continues, just like me!
A clam tells stories of its great fight,
While starfish giggles, oh what a sight!

Sunburnt tourists brought snacks galore,
Seagulls plot heists; they're never a bore.
With sun hats crooked, we laugh and scream,
The beach is a stage for our wacky dream.

The sand tickles toes, like a playful tease,
And jellyfish float like silly tease.
We reenact pirates, all dressed in rags,
While crabs throw shade, in clever jags.

As waves crash down, our laughter flies,
Into the blue, beneath sunny skies.
A day full of jest, forever to savor,
In this coastal charm, we find our favor.

Symphony of the Sunlit Sea

Surfboards line up for a surf-off show,
With flips and falls, it's pure comic gold.
Seals clap their flippers, cheering for fun,
As we tumble and splash in the warm sun.

The sea sings loudly, a bubbly tune,
While dolphins giggle, dancing like loons.
Waves do a rumba, oh what a scene,
As we all join in, feeling like queens!

Each tumble's a story, each wipeout a laugh,
Collecting our giggles on a watery path.
Our hair's like seaweed, wild and free,
And sunscreen's a fight, just wait and see.

As the day ends with a sunset glory,
We gather to share our splashing story.
To the tune of the sea, we dance, we sway,
In this silly symphony, we'll always stay.

Echoes of the Gentle Surfers

Surfers unite for a grand old time,
Chasing each wave like it's a crime.
With boards that wobble and tails that flip,
A parade of blunders, a comedic trip.

We dodge the surf with an awkward grace,
Falling like fish; oh, what a race!
The ocean giggles, teasing our fate,
As we carve our names on the sea, it's fate.

Sun-kissed and salty, we rise with glee,
With moonlit tacos, it's how we'll be.
Riding the waves with laughter in store,
Each splash brings echoes, a call to explore.

So join the fun, no need to be shy,
Grab a board, give it a try!
In this crazy world of surf and play,
The echoes of laughter will always stay.

Charm of the Coastline's Soft Serenade

Seagulls squawk as they steal my fries,
Shells like treasures beneath sunny skies.
Waves giggle and whisper, oh what a spree,
Every splash is a dance, come join the glee!

Boys in the surf try to surf on their boards,
But end up just flopping like confused little lords.
The lifeguard snores, sunbathing in style,
While dolphins pass by with a cheeky smile.

Sandcastles crumble with a mighty boom,
As kids shriek with joy, we'll need a vacuum!
Ice cream cones drip like a melting dream,
Every single scoop has its own little theme.

The beach ball bounces, oh what a sight,
A toddler trips over and starts a delight.
With laughter and splashes, the shoreline beams,
For this is the place where a humorist dreams.

An Oasis of Soft Whispers

Under the sun, we lounge on the sand,
A crab in a hat, oh so terribly grand.
With laughter as tall as the waves we chase,
The tide just rolled in to crash at our pace!

Umbrellas compete for the biggest flair,
As sunscreen warriors fight off the glare.
Kids screaming in joy, chasing their dreams,
While the beach ball wobbles—oh, how it beams!

A picnic spread out, but who ate the pie?
It vanished so quick, oh my, oh my!
With seagulls squawking a comical tune,
We jump with each wave, just like a cartoon!

In this oasis, our worries do flee,
Life's a little silly, and that's just the key.
With each shared laugh, our breadcrumbs remain,
As fun on the coastline flows like the rain.

Serene Soliloquies by the Shore

Whispers of ocean, oh what a tease,
The fish are all laughing, caught in the breeze.
My flip-flops fly off with a flinging twist,
And the tide ponders how I'll ever coexist.

I build my grand castle, a real work of art,
But the waves conspire and tear it apart.
With a bucket in hand, I take my sweet time,
While crabs bust a move, oh what a wild rhyme!

The sunburned tourists in search of some shade,
Look up with confusion, a big ice cream trade.
While laughter erupts from a water balloon,
Floating gently, like dreams, under the moon!

As the day turns to dusk with colors aglow,
We dance with our shadows, oh what a show.
In serene soliloquies, our hearts sing,
The shoreline holds secrets that happiness brings.

The Art of Living in the Moment

Flip-flops squeak as I dance in the sand,
I wave to a crab—it waves back, isn't it grand?
A sunscreen mishap leaves me quite silly,
I'm a walking ghost, all globby and frilly!

As I chase after seagulls to steal my snack,
They plot with the tide, planning their attack.
Kids shout with glee, building towers so tall,
Until a wave crashes down—oh, what a fall!

The ice cream vendor strikes a comical pose,
But it slips from his hand, oh where does it go?
For laughter is tasty and sunshine's a feast,
Our moments become memories, shared with the least.

The art of the present, where giggles abound,
With every small splash, joy can be found.
In the dance of the waves and the salt in the air,
We live for today, without any care!

Mysterious Currents

The water's a jester, with waves that do dance,
It tickles our toes, like a playful romance.
Fish wear tiny hats, as they swim in a line,
We laugh as they waltz, oh, isn't it divine?

Seagulls wear sunglasses, so chic and so bright,
They strut on the sand, in a comical sight.
Crabs snap and they pinch, join the crazy parade,
While we sip our drinks, under sun's masquerade.

The tide comes a-callin', with jellyfish pranks,
They drift through the sea like colorful tanks.
Who knew the ocean had such funny flair?
A comedy show performed in salt air!

So let's raise a toast, to this zany affair,
With laughter and joy, let's breathe in the air.
For life by the sea is a laugh every day,
With waterside antics that brighten our play.

Hidden Shores

On the quest for treasure, we dig in the sand,
Finding seashells and seaweed, isn't it grand?
A crab gave a wink, borrowed mom's best hat,
Said, "I wear it well—what do you think of that?"

Waves whisper secrets, they giggle and roar,
While starfish in tuxedos check their watch on the shore.
"Time for a dance!" said a clam with a grin,
As the octopus joined, let the party begin!

So let's catch the tide, with pails full of dreams,
Designing our castles with sand, oh, it seems.
Our moats are the rivers, our flags made of foam,
The beach is our kingdom, oh how I feel at home!

With laughter echoing, and joy in the air,
We'll celebrate life, without a single care.
For every funny moment spent under the sun,
These hidden shores promise the best kind of fun!

Horizons of Bliss Underneath Starlit Skies

Stars twinkle brightly, like disco balls spun,
We dance on the beach, laughing just for fun.
The moon joins the party, wearing shades of gold,
While sand crabs start busting their moves, bold and old.

The breeze whispers jokes, tickling our nose,
As tides sway and shimmer, in this nighttime show.
The dolphins put on a splashy gentle spree,
"Come dance with us now!" they chirp gleefully.

With cool ocean breezes, our hearts feel so light,
As we toast to the stars, shining joyous and bright.
Why's it always so funny when the night comes alive?
Because laughter and friends are what help us survive!

So here's to the magic, beneath twilight's gleam,
Where giggles and dreams flow smoother than cream.
Let's cherish these moments that dance in our eyes,
As we weave through the night, under vast velvet skies.

Driftwood Poems in a Seaside Haiku

Driftwood tells a tale,
Of mischief in the surf,
With laughter afloat.

Seashells gossip soft,
Whispers of a silly dance,
Under moonlit charm.

Waves crash like a tune,
Rhythms of a joyful song,
Heartbeats sync with foam.

Sandy feet tap fast,
Crab joins in the conga line,
The tide winks with glee.

Tides Whispering Secrets of the Night

The moon paints the waves in a shimmering glow,
As the tide tells secrets, they ebb and they flow.
A turtle in top hat, quite dapper and grand,
Pinches his tailfin, says, "Join this weird band!"

The fish are all giggling, they leap through the air,
With splashes and bubbles, who else could compare?
A party of crabs in bow ties and flair,
Form a dance troupe, with moves beyond fair.

The jellyfish float by, with lights all aglow,
They twirl like a dancer, putting on quite the show.
The seaweed forms wigs, for those feeling brave,
In this nighttime gala, we all misbehave!

As stars wink above, we dance till we tire,
Finding joy in the waves, lifting hearts even higher.
So here's to the night, with laughter in store,
Under tides that keep sharing their secrets galore!

Whispers of the Tidal Breeze

The seagulls squawk, they steal my fries,
As sunburned tourists wear goofy ties.
With sand in shoes, we laugh and roam,
Who knew the beach could feel like home?

The crabs do a dance, all sideways and quick,
While surfers tumble; oh, what a trick!
Beach balls collide with laughter and cheer,
I think I just swallowed some saltwater beer!

A kid builds a castle, grand and immense,
But a wave rolls in, oh, what a suspense!
It crumbles and splashes, he starts to shout,
"Mom! I promise, I built it about!"

The sun sets low, the sky turns gold,
As I moonwalk in sand, feeling quite bold.
With ice cream drips and laughter that gleam,
Life's just a frolic, a sweet summer dream.

Dancing Shadows on Sandy Shores

Under the sun, the shadows play,
With beach umbrellas swaying, oh, what a display!
Flip-flops flapping, the fun's out of hand,
Someone's phone gets buried in the sand!

Children are chasing, almost on cue,
The ice cream truck that rolls right on through.
Melty delights become sticky affairs,
As we trade silly looks and wild stares.

In pirate hats, we shout "Arrr!" and cheer,
Scaring away any lurking fear.
With coconuts clinking, we toast with delight,
To the funniest adventures, both day and night!

As shadows grow long, we dance with glee,
Sandcastles crumble; oh, look at me!
With laughter that echoes, the night takes form,
Under the starry sky, our spirits warm.

Echoes of Celestial Waves

The ocean whispers jokes, oh so sly,
As dolphins giggle, leaping high.
With salty air and sandy toes,
We roll like waves, in gleeful throes.

A fisherman's hat flies into the sea,
Forgetting his bait, oh silly me!
The beach ball bounces, escapes with a grin,
Who knew aquatic laughter could cause such a spin?

Turtles in shades cruise by with a flair,
Sipping on coconut milk, without a care.
With a wink and a nudge, they glide on their way,
Joining our antics at the end of the day!

Under the stars, we gather and jest,
Sharing our tales of the ocean's best.
With every chuckle, our hearts take flight,
In the embrace of whimsy, we dance through the night.

The Lullaby of Salty Winds

The breeze sings soft, its tune quite absurd,
Whispers of surf, a comical word.
While beach bums snooze, hats over their eyes,
A crab pulls a prank; oh my, what a surprise!

Towels and sunblock scatter and fly,
A seagull descends, swoops down from the sky.
With chips in its beak, it struts like a king,
A seaside performance, pure comedy's fling!

A pie on the table, lurking so near,
A child swipes a slice, grinning ear to ear.
With pie faces round, and giggles galore,
Who knew a beach could deliver such lore?

As the stars sparkle bright, we sing our own tune,
Beneath a coconut tree, under the moon.
The salty winds laugh, as dreams take their flight,
We dance with our shadows, embracing the night.

www.ingramcontent.com/pod-product-compliance
Lightning Source LLC
Chambersburg PA
CBHW072121070526
44585CB00016B/1517